ADVENTURER PARROT
LORY

ADVENTURER PARROT LORY

Mustafa Yılmaz

Translator:
İbrahim Ögel

1th Edition

September - 2024

ISBN: **978-625-98442-0-6**

Editor: **Yasemin Çınar**
Cover Design & Illustration: **Fatma Karaoğlan**
Layout: DIZGI**MIZANPAJ**.COM

İKİ EYLÜL YAYINEVİ
Piyade Mahallesi 1681. Cadde No: 80/6 Etimesgut - Ankara
0546 426 21 84
www.ikieylulyayinevi.com.tr
ikieylulyayinevi@gmail.com
ikieylulyayinevi

ADVENTURER PARROT LORY

Mustafa Yılmaz

Translator: İbrahim Ögel

CHAPTER 1: FOREST FELLOWS

With the sunrise, the forest slowly began to live. The inhabitants of the forest came out of their nests, one by one. They turned their faces to the sky as if greeting the sun. They had left the difficult winter behind. Sprouts of leaves, heralds of spring, had bloomed on the branches of the trees. The ground was decorated with flowers of many colors. Colorful butterflies emerged from their cocoons and landed on the flowers. The cubs born in winter are now grown up. While they were walking around with their mothers, they were also getting to know plants and living things.

The forest fellows were like a big family. Many different kinds of creatures lived there. The habits of living together for years had made them friends.

They would go out in search of food early every morning and return to their nests before evening. And they would share the food they found with their offspring.

This morning, they woke up to the food that nature had prepared for them. One of them was Lory's mother and father. Until they arrived, he would leave his nest and perch on nearby trees. He would play with parrots that were like her and make friends with them.

Jako, Arya and Tuty were his best friends. He spent the most time with them. What they loved most was to open their wings and show off the colors they had. Lory had the most color. His head was blue, his body was green, the shoulders of his wings were yellow, and the lower part was blue. His tail was red.

Tuty's chest was red and the rest was green. Arya's chest was yellow and everywhere else was blue.

Jako had the plainest color among them. Every part of him was gray except for his tail. He had a short tail. That was red too.

During the day, they would leap on the high branches of trees. They would take off for a bit and then land again. They would perform these movements over and over again. They would have fun and strengthen their wings.

They would help each other to eat the fruits. Sometimes they would drop it on the branch of the tree, sometimes they would drop it on the ground and eat it like that. They loved bananas and pineapples. In the evening, they would eat the seeds brought by their parents.

CHAPTER 2: FOREIGN GUEST

One day, a fledgling came to the area where their tree was located. It was obvious that he came from far away. They were a little scared because it was their first time seeing a different type of bird.

This bird had a different appearance than them. He had a small head and a pointed beak like a hook. He had a sharp and harsh look. He didn't have vibrant colors like them. He had a brown, matte tone. There was only a few white patches on the inside of his wings. But despite all this, The Fledgling caught the attention of Lory and her friends. They looked at The Fledgling with curious eyes. The fledgling also noticed that they were looking at him.

"Hello, my name is Cesur," he said. "I come from far away. "When I was tired, I wanted to rest here for a while."

"Hello, welcome," said Lory. Then Arya, Jako and Tuty also said 'hello'. Lory was confused because he had never seen a bird like this before. He wanted to satisfy his curiosity as soon as possible.

"Cesur, this is the first time we see a bird like you. "What species of birds are you from?" he said.

"I'm a fledgling," said Cesur.

Lory opened his right wing and said:

"We always live here. This is our home in winter and summer. "We never migrated."

"Actually, we do not always migrate. But sometimes we migrate due to natural conditions. Thanks to this migration, we see many different places. We meet many different creatures. Since many bird species also migrate, we make friends during our journey. "We eat foods with different tastes," said Cesur.

Thereupon, a desire to see new places and meet different creatures arose in Lory's heart. He dreamed of meeting more birds. He dreamed of eating delicious fruits. Meanwhile, when his mouth started to drool, he licked the edge of his beak with his little tongue.

"How far away do you come from?" "Are these places you are describing very far away?"

"Actually, it's not that far away. You have grown up now. If you can fly comfortably, you can go back and forth without getting tired. It will be a good experience for you too. This way, you will gain new experiences."

Lory turned his head to Arya after Cesur's words. He looked at her as if to say what are you thinking? Arya realized that Lory was affected by

Cesur's words. She realized that he, too, wanted to go to other lands like Cesur.

After a while, Cesur asked permission from Lory and her friends. He had rested enough. He had to continue on his way now. After saying goodbye, he flew into the sky through the trees.

Jako, looking after Cesur, turned to his friends and said:

"Maybe next year we can go to see new places," he said. Tuty moved his head up and down and said:

"We eat very good food," he said. Then he kept up the pace by saying 'I want, I want'. Everyone's joy increased even more. Others, like Tuty, move their heads up and down:

They kept up the pace, saying, "We want it, we want it!"

Towards evening, Lory's parents returned home. Arya also saw her own family coming. Immediately afterwards, Jako and Tuty also saw their families return. They each said goodbye and left the tree where they had landed.

Lory's parents brought a branch with seeds. Lory didn't realize he was hungry. But when he saw the seeds, his mouth drool.

After dinner, his mother asked what they did today. Arya said that Cesur came while she was playing with Jako and Tuty.

"Who do you call Cesur, my child?" said his mother.

''He was coming from far away. He stopped by our forest while migrating to other places. He needed some rest," Lory said.

His father knew that foreign birds sometimes visited the forest. He wondered what species it was.

"Well, my dear, did this Cesur tell you what kind of bird he was?"

"Yes, daddy," she said. He was a fledgling bird. He had a tiny head. The tip of its beak was also very sharp."

His mother and father were a little uneasy. Because fledglings were from the predatory family. They did not get along well with parrotlets.

"I also had my friends with me. We had a very nice chat. "He told us that he saw many different places, made friends with different kinds of creatures, and most importantly, he told he ate very good food."

CHAPTER 3: JOURNEY TO DREAMS

Lory couldn't sleep that night. He thought about what Cesur had told her throughout the night. He had always been curious about distant places. 'Who were there, what was their life like?' He asked a lot of questions. He often dreamed. His dream was to fly high in the sky one day. He wanted to perch on the top of the lofty mountains, whose heads reached up to the clouds. He dreamed of listening to the sounds of big waterfalls and getting wet in those waters. He would left himself to the deep blue seas.

Lory went to Arya early in the morning. He told her about the journey he was thinking about last night. He wanted to travel like a Cesur. In this way, he would try to increase his knowledge and culture. He wanted Arya to accompany him on this journey.

Arya explained that such a long journey could be full of dangers. She said that they have not yet gone to an area other than their own forest.

"You are right in what you said. Traveling, seeing and tasting different things are very nice feelings. But we don't know what to face, right? "It's a very risky journey, it could harm us," said Arya.

But Lory was persistent and determined. He was willing to face all kinds of dangers. He was going to fly and achieve his dreams.

"I'm determined, Arya. Of course, I will have some trouble and encounter difficulties. Otherwise, how can I do all this? Besides, I won't do it just for myself. I will be an example to all the parrots in the forest. "I will do it for them too."

He also told his parents about his desire to

go on a journey. They also objected like Arya. But they could not dissuade Lory from this wish. They finally let him go.

After saying goodbye to Arya, Jako and Tuty, he spread his wings wide. He took off high above the trees in the forest. He enjoyed the air entering between the feathers on his wings. The happiness he felt was reflected on his face. While floating in the air, he looked down at one point. The forest where he was born and raised looked so small.

CHAPTER 4: THE ADVENTURE BEGINS

Lory flew in the sky for hours. He was in great mood. He didn't even think about being tired. Towards evening, he started looking for a place to sleep. There were huge trees nearby that remained lush green. There was a cold stream flowing from the peaks of the mountain. There were sounds of splashing water. Lory sat on the branch of a tree and began to watch all the beauty. There were also fruits that he wanted. The sun was slowly setting before his eyes. It had turned a red. The beauty of the view fascinated Lory.

But suddenly the wind started blowing. Then it got more and more intense. The branches of the trees were swinging from side to side. The clouds increased and it started to get dark. Light-

ning flashed repeatedly. It stretched like a long line from the sky to the ground. With each flash of lightning, the place was illuminated. Beforehand, thunder booms were shaking everywhere. And then the heavy rain started and continued without stopping.

Lory's heart began to pound. He was experiencing the shock of the sudden rain. Every part of his body was wet. Their feathers were stuck together due to the rain. He couldn't hold on to the tree he landed on. The branches had become very slippery. He immediately started looking for shelter. He took shelter in the empty hollow of the tree in front of him. He looked around to see if there were anyone else around. But there was no one else but him.

His feathers, wet with rain, had become unable to protect him from the cold. He was cold.

Evening was starting to take effect and the weather was getting darker. After a while, the rain stopped. There was a deep silence.

Lory poked his head out of his hiding place. He looked around again. He looked in the hope of seeing someone. But there was no one. He walked to a dry corner of the cave. He closed her eyes with the consolation that at least he had a place to spend the night.

CHAPTER 5: MONKEY PAMPU

The sun rising in the early hours began to make its heat felt. Lory came out of the hole where he spent the night and landed on a high branch. He spread his wings to both sides and began to dry his wet feathers. The warmth of the sun was comforting. While he thought he was slowly drying himself off, drops of water fell on his head from above. When he looked up he saw a little baby monkey. The baby monkey jumped from branch to branch with its long arms and came to Lory. On the other hand, he was eating the banana in his hand. Without taking his eyes off Lory:

"What are you doing here?" he said in a confused manner. "This is the first time I see a bird like you."

Lory was happy to see such a relaxed attitude of the baby monkey because he felt him friendly.

"Hello, I am a parrot. "I come from far away," he said. After straining the monkey:

"My name is Lory. "Do you have a name?" He said.

"Of course I have. How did you know I have not? "I'm Pampu."

"Pumpu?"

"No, Pampu," he repeated.

"Pampu, Pampu..."

"Yes dear, don't you like it?"

"No.. Don't think like that. I like it a lot. But this is the first time I hear such a name."

"Why did you go so far from home?" said Pampu.

Pampu's question reminded Lory of her home, family, friends and especially Arya. 'The journey can be fraught with danger,' he remembered. Even though he was only at the beginning of his journey, he missed them very much.

"I..." he said, swallowing. After pausing for a while:

"I went on a long journey to see new places, make new friends and eat different tastes of food."

Pampu started to wander among the branches of the trees again. He jumped from the branch and held on to a banana tree. He plucked a banana and returned to Lory.

Lory liked Pampu's acrobatic moves. His effortless stance even on the thinnest branches impressed him.

Pampu held out the banana in Lory's hand and said:

"You must be hungry, take this banana," he said and placed it in front of Lory.

"Thank you very much, I was very hungry," he said. And he started peeling the banana with his beak. He held the banana with one foot to prevent it from falling. Lory thanked him after eating the banana given by Pampu.

Pampu, upon Lory eating the banana with appetite:

"If you want, I can tell you where there is more fruit and food. You will even meet many different creatures," he said. My father goes there from time to time and tells me about what he sees.

"I would love to. It would be very good for me."

Pampu showed Lory the way to go and wished him luck. Lory also said he was very happy to meet him. He left Pampu, saying that he would stop by again if he happened to be in the way. He took off towards the sky, flapping his wings rapidly.

CHAPTER 6: WISE RABBIT KALPCAN

While Lory was floating in the air, he saw a rabbit among the rocks. He had many rabbit friends in the forest where he lived before. He remembered the days when he played with them. They would imitate many animals with their parrot friends.

Just the sounds of animals? They would imitate everything they heard. Sometimes it's the whoosh, whoosh, whoosh sound of a blowing wind, and sometimes it's the whoop, whoop, whoop sound of drops falling from the leaves into the puddle after the rain...

Remembering the old days, he floated towards the area where the rabbit was located. But the rabbit suddenly started running. As Lory's shadow got closer, the rabbit was getting faster. Lory was very surprised. He couldn't make sense of the rabbit's sudden acceleration. He accelerated to catch up and was out of breath.

Finally the rabbit went into a hole beyond the rocks. Lory landed in a tree across from the hole. It was the first time in his life that he flew so fast. His heart was pounding as if it was about to burst out of its place.

After taking a breather, he called to the rabbit:

"Hey! Brother rabbit, why are you running away from me? "I wanted to come to you to talk to you."

Hearing Lory's voice, the rabbit realized that he was a parrot. He came out of the hole where he took shelter in fear. There was actually a parrot standing in front of him. But what would a parrot be doing here?

Standing on its two hind legs:

"You scared me. When I suddenly saw your shadow in front of me..."

Lory said embarassedly:

"I didn't mean to scare you. "I just wanted to talk," he said. And with the desire to meet:

"I'm Lory," he said.

"And I am Kalp Can," rabbit said. I thought you were a hawk following me. It has been after me for a few days. After staring Lory for a while:

"And what is a parrot like you doing here? You rarely come here. At that time, the adults come in flocks," he said.

Lory talked about the forest where he lived, his family, and his friends. He told how he set out on the journey, taking the fledgling Cesur as an example.

Rabbit Kalp Can listened to Lory with great sincerity. He asked about the situation of his rabbit brothers in the forest where Lory lived. He learned that they, too, lived a cautious life like him.

Then he started talking about where he lived. It covered a wide area extending from the foothills of the mountains to the plain. Unlike forests, they were places where there were open areas.

"This place where I live is also close to people's living spaces. Sometimes they come after us too," said Kalp Can.

What Kalp Can told made Lory nervous. With a serious facial expression:

"So what do people want from you?" he said.

Rabbit Kalp Can brought many memories before his eyes with the maturity of his age and experience. He remembered the days when he lived among people. He remembered how well the man-cub had treated him after he was captured. The food he gave was piled up to the top. Getting rid of the deep memories he was immersed in,

"Some want to be loved, some want to be with them like a friend," he said. Smiling at Lory's ignorance of this situation:

"They keep not only us, but also almost many animals with them."

"Are they behaving badly?"

"No... On the contrary, they behave very well. They feed well. But what can replace the freedom in nature?

After this conversation, they both felt a bit calm. Then Kalp Can looked at the path below the cliff and said:

"Dude Lory, I have to go now. I went a long way from my nest because of the hawk. "A long road awaits me," he said.

Lory thanked Kalp Can for this nice conversation. He said that he would not forget the information he gave him.

Kalp Can stood up on both feet and greeted Lory. And he turned onto the path and started running quickly.

The moment Lory took off to fly, the question he forgot to ask Kalp Can came to his mind:

"Which direction would he go?"

CHAPTER 7: CAGE

Lory surveyed the surroundings. He saw that there was a river bed some distance away. He flew towards the river, hoping to drink clean water and find someone who could give him directions.

When he reached the river, he saw nothing but fish jumping occasionally on the water. He felt the slight coldness of the water on a large stone he had placed on. He started looking around to find something. He noticed that there were things looked like grains of seeds under the tree nearby.

He turned towards the seeds to suppress his hunger and regain some strength. It was just the

right thing for him. It was the first time he was eating hearty food since he started the journey.

What he ate was so delicious that he passed out. He continued to eat all the seeds without stopping.

But suddenly he saw something coming towards him from the branches of the tree. When he realized what happened, it was too late, he was caught in a big net.

He started to flutter, lifting his wings with all his might. But he was helpless against the big and heavy net.

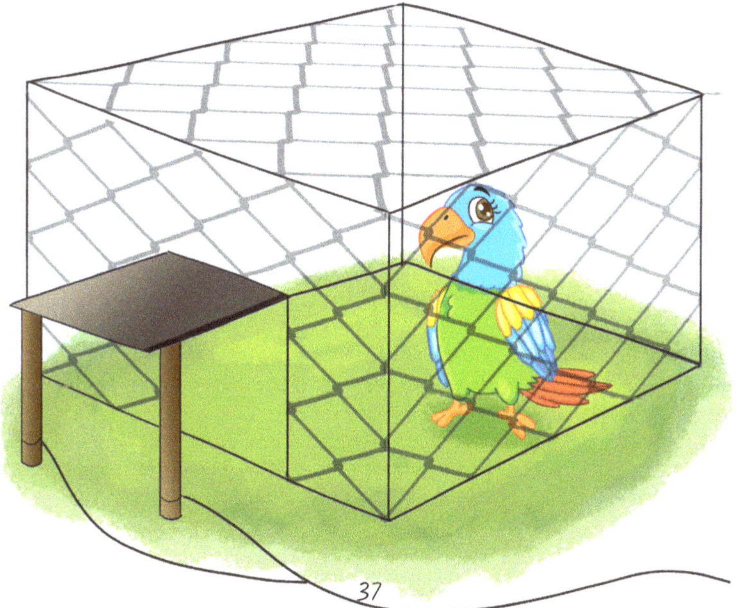

He started to hear footsteps ahead. The voices gradually grew louder. And when the voices finally stopped, there were two feet in boots in front of him. He was caught in a trap set by a hunter.

The man left the cage he brought with him next to the net. He took Lory from the net and put it in the cage. And he began to walk calmly and confidently towards his home on the farm.

Lory looked through the swinging cage to the tree he had just been caught in. He was getting smaller with each passing step.

Just like he experienced when he left home. How small the forest seemed to him that day.